The Jewish-Christian Connection
An Interfaith Experience

The
Jewish-Christian
Connection

An Interfaith Experience

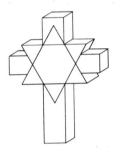

Devin-Adair, Publishers
Greenwich, Connecticut

Manufactured in the United States of America.

Logo by Kenneth J. Roberts

Library of Congress Cataloging-in-Publication Data

Bishop, John W.
 The Jewish-Christian connection.

 1. Judaism—Relations—Christianity. 2. Christianity and other religions—Judaism. 3. Interfaith worship—Connecticut—Greenwich. 4. Greenwhich (Conn.)—Religious life and customs. I. Silverman, Hillel E., 1924– II. Yaseen, Leonard, 1912–. III. Title.
BM535.B525 1987 261.2'6'097469 86-24051
ISBN 0-8159-5903-6

Devin-Adair, Publishers
Excellence, Since 1911

Contents

Introduction 7

The Religious Organizations 9

Testimonies To Faith 13

Did You Know? 16

The Easter-Passover Connection 19

When Neighbors Get Together 27

The Jewish-Christian Connection 36

The Next Step: What You Can Do 50

The Contributors 51

Last Words: 56

   From the Psalms of David 56

   From the Proverbs of Solomon 58

   Matthew 5:23, 24 59

   The Lord's Prayer 59

Acknowledgment 61

Introduction

This book describes a remarkable interfaith weekend shared by two congregations of differing religious perspectives: Temple Sholom and Christ Episcopal Church in Greenwich, Connecticut. They have existed side by side for many years and while relationships were cordial, it seemed to the clergy and laity that more could be done to promote brotherhood, mutual respect and understanding.

Consequently we designed a weekend together to be called "When Neighbors Get Together—The Jewish-Christian Connection and the Passover-Easter Connection."

On Friday evening members of Christ Church attended the weekly service at Temple Sholom at which the Rev. Dr. John Bishop delivered the sermon on the topic of Easter. After service we joined together for refreshments and Israeli folk dancing.

On Sunday morning the members of Temple Sholom attended service at Christ Church where Rabbi Silverman gave the sermon on the topic of Passover. At each of the two services of worship, the liturgy was conducted as always so each congregation could experience the other's traditional forms. Following service on Sunday the large assembly of Christians and Jews gathered in the Social Hall to attend the lecture by the author Leonard Yaseen whose recent book *The Jesus Connection* has been receiving wide acclaim.

The Religious Organizations

The first Episcopal service in Greenwich was held in 1705 under the auspices of the Church of England. In 1747–49 Horseneck Chapel (in those days the center of Greenwich was known as Horseneck) was built by Greenwich Episcopalians. The Chapel became a mission of St. John's Church, Stamford, originally a mission of Christ's Church, Rye, New York, and services were conducted by the Rev. Ebenezer Dibble, Rector of St. John's.

By 1834, having weathered the American Revolution, reestablished its historic links to the Church of England—thanks to Samuel Seabury, Connecticut's first bishop—and established itself as a full member of the now independent Episcopal Church of the United States, Christ Church not only had a new building with a belfry, but was for the first time a full-fledged parish.

Over the years Christ Church has been instrumental in founding five other Episcopal congregations in Greenwich, two of which are still thriving. Three of Christ Church's rectors went on to become bishops of the Episcopal Church of the United States. It is the largest Christian church in Greenwich, and among the largest Episcopal churches in Connecticut, with over 2,500 baptized members. Christ Church has long been a leader in ecumenical relations in the community.

* * *

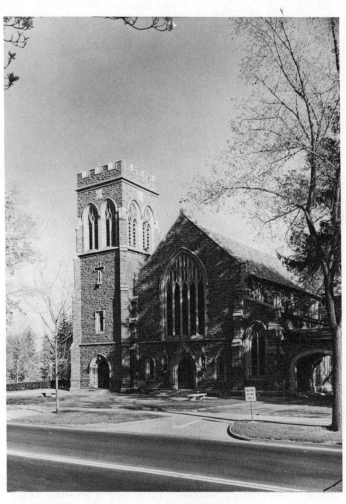

Christ Church, Greenwich, Connecticut
(Credit: Elemer Kardos, Norwalk, CT)

Temple Sholom, Greenwich, Connecticut

Seventy years ago ten Jewish families who lived and worked in Greenwich decided to create their own spiritual home and rented Abrams Hall on Greenwich Avenue where they conducted High Holy services and arranged for the Hebrew education of their children.

In 1919 the group was officially incorporated as

the Greenwich Hebrew Institute, and by 1921 they had purchased a building at 23 Elm Street. A Ladies Auxiliary, forerunner of the present Sisterhood, was formed in 1924, and weekly Sabbath services were begun in 1925. In 1931 the cemetery on Riversville Road was purchased and in 1934 the first Congregational Seder was held.

During the mid-1930s and into the 1940s the Greenwich Hebrew Institute confirmed its first class, established a Jewish Welfare Fund and held pulpit exchanges with Protestant clergy. During World War II Rabbi Meyer Miller became a chaplain and many of the congregation's sons went to war.

In the post-war era Greenwich Jews joined the commitment to the creation of the State of Israel. Having outgrown their Elm Street home, the congregation began a building fund in 1948 and by 1955 Temple Sholom was dedicated at its present location on Putnam Avenue.

Through the years the Temple has sought to teach others about Judaism with such events as a Hanukkah Music Festival and an Israeli Art Show and sale. Always involved in community affairs, it continues to expand its devotion to local welfare projects. Today, Temple Sholom has a thriving Hebrew School, and a highlight of its program year is a series featuring guest performers from every field of Jewish cultural endeavor.

Testimonies to Faith

"No one participating in the interfaith weekend could have failed to become more aware of the closeness of our neighboring congregations as they shared in the hope, joy and power of the Lord."

Elly Parker

"It was the single greatest theological experience I've had in ten years of religious doings in Greenwich. If other congregations emulate this weekend's actions, I believe there is hope for brotherhood and tolerance."

Roger H. Lourie

"It is hard to capture the spirit that pervaded last spring's ecumenical weekend. One can only hope that the warmth and joy of those few days have set a tone for many years to come."

Rebecca S. Breed

"The sermons by Rabbi Silverman and the Rev. John W. Bishop and the address by Leonard Yaseen brought about a better understanding between Christians and Jews. Our worship together has created interest and caring between both faiths."

Richard G. Slagle

"I'm not so naïve as to think we will eradicate the long-existing mistakes and misunderstandings, but let us pray (together!) that we will continue in the climate and steps taken this weekend. . . . People need leaders and [Rabbi Silverman and Dr. Bishop] are giving this to us and for this we praise the Lord."

Dorothy Karrel

"We were enriched beyond measure and shall long remember the outreach of our neighbors, made real and personal by the model . . . held up for all the community to see."

Joel Hirsch

"What a meaningful weekend [Dr. Bishop and Rabbi Silverman] gave to me. Ever since I was a little girl I have yearned to know more about the Jewish faith and customs. I was never taught prejudice, but I never had a chance to share faith with a Jewish friend. . . . It was a warm and exciting time for me to be at the Friday evening service and to have [the Temple Sholom congregation] with us on Sunday. . . . [I am grateful] for the time, effort and the love put into providing a weekend of brotherhood for us. I hope it can be an annual event."

Eleen Hubbard

"I join in thanking God for His many blessings. Being part of the service at the Episcopal Church was a great joy for me, and [I am grateful] for the endeavors for unity among all peoples."

Sr. Margaret Hoban

Did You Know?

- In the first century the Jewish people, oppressed by the brutal Roman Empire, stood alone as monotheists among pagan nations.

- To many Jews, Jesus of Nazareth was the person who could overthrow Roman domination. Jesus was of the tribe of Judah, linked to David, Abraham and Moses. A Jewish mother, Mary, nursed him.

- Jesus was born, lived and died as a Jew. The only bible Jesus read was the Hebrew bible and the prophets of Israel. His teachings were based on Hebrew scriptures.

- The Jews did not collectively reject Jesus. His disciples were all Jews. So were John the Baptist and all the early bishops and saints. His fellow Jews respected and accepted him as a teacher and leader.

- While Jews were sympathetic to Jesus as a Messiah, their own commitment to a unique God in heaven made it impossible for them to accept Jesus's divinity. Many Jews felt they could not join Paul's new sect for this reason.

- For forty years after Jesus's death Jewish-Christian worship services were often held in synagogues. Christian services are patterned on synagogue customs.

- The concepts of heaven and hell, the Psalms, the terms amen and hallelujah, baptism, and the Lord's Prayer all stem from Jewish beliefs. The Last Supper was a Passover celebration.

- Christians were treated barbarically and were totally dependent on Roman authorities for their existence. Persecution of Christianity was continuous: Churches were demolished, Christians were burned at the stake, religious documents were confiscated. It was not until the fourth century, under Emperor Constantine, that Christianity was actively encouraged.

- Over time, religious instruction conditioned successive generations with mythical arguments. Over time, these myths became accepted as events that happened exactly as portrayed.

- The notion that the Jews are collectively responsible for the death of Jesus, their fellow Jew, is one of these myths. The Gospels have numerous sections that indicate that Jews were not wholly responsible for his death.

- Jesus's Jewish followers loved and accepted him. Jesus was not put on trial before the Supreme Court of Judea. Under Jewish law, he had committed no crime.

- Two persons share most of the responsibility for Jesus's crucifixion: the Jewish high priest Caiaphas, and the Roman procurator Pontius Pilate.

- Caiaphas was hated by the Jews. As a Roman collaborator, he was not a true Jewish leader. He was appointed by Rome, served at the behest of Rome, and was instructed by Roman authorities, who had enslaved the Jewish people.

- Pontius Pilate was a rapacious and cruel brute, recognized for corruptibility and violence. He lined the roads of Judea with crucified Jews.

    –From *The Jesus Connection* by Leonard Yaseen

The Easter-Passover Connection

I'd like to begin by saying how very nice it was of Pope John Paul, last weekend, to visit the synagogue in Rome, to pave the way for our weekend of shared visits here in Greenwich. And as Hillel mentioned to me a few days ago, while it may be true that this is the first Pope ever to visit a synagogue in Rome (or anywhere else), it's also true that I am the first Bishop ever to visit Temple Sholom in Greenwich.

And may I say seriously what a very great pleasure it is for me to be here to share in your worship and I know I also speak for others. One of the things I share with the Pope (and there are not many things I do share with him) is that this, too, is my first time to officially visit a Jewish temple. I have, of course, been in your building unofficially many times before—mostly when I come to pick up Rabbi Silverman for our weekly tennis game. However, that is not exactly an ecumenical or spiritual event although I have noticed that Rabbi prays a lot during our game.

Actually, perhaps I misspoke myself when I said I have not been here officially before. As you know, some months ago Rabbi Silverman and I and officials of our two congregations conducted a liturgy together out in your parking lot. We presided over the removal of those three great stones which literally separated our parking lots and symbolically separated our congregations. These rocks dominated that area which had come to be known as the Gaza Strip.

As I think about that episode of the stones, I am reminded of the great text from the Book of Joshua, when God said to Joshua as the people passed over the Jordan: "Take twelve stones from the river and carry them with you" (Joshua 4:5) and, "And when your children ask, what do these stones mean to you, ye shall reply . . . they will be a memorial . . ." (Joshua 4:7)

Those *three* stones are now removed and sitting by the side of the driveway, and when our children ask, "What do these stones mean?" we can all say that they are a sort of symbol, not any longer of separation, but of the friendship and shared life of our two congregations. That is really what this weekend is all about—an expression of our friendship and our shared faith and witness to the one true God and Father of us all.

Actually, as you all know, the connection between our two congregations goes very far back: The first Christ Church, called Horseneck Chapel, stood on this plot of ground in 1748, and remained for many years until destroyed by a great storm. When the Temple was built here in the 1950s that move was strongly supported and applauded by Christ Church and its then Rector, the Rev. Robert Appleyard. Bob Appleyard is remembered as having seen the Temple next door to Christ Church as the fulfillment of the scriptures: Old Testament and New Testament standing side by side. Certainly we the Christians are richer by your presence—and we hope vice versa as well.

When Bob Appleyard left Christ Church in 1965 to go to a parish in Florida, the people of Temple Sholom presented him this scroll:

> In recognition and gratitude for
> the ministry of the Rev. Robert
> Appleyard of Christ Church, Greenwich,
> the people of Temple Sholom, Greenwich,
> have caused 100 trees to be planted in
> the land of Israel.

Bob Appleyard reported just recently that he and his wife were in Israel not long ago and they hoped to see the trees. They stood in front of a literal forest of trees and said, "We don't know which ones were given by Temple Sholom but it is a great thrill to know that those special 100 trees are out there somewhere."

As Hillel Silverman and I thought about and helped plan this weekend together, we were reminded again and again that the profound connection between Judaism and Christianity cannot be overstated. Whether it is the Jesus connection, the Passover-Easter connection, the scriptures, our shared liturgies, our common spiritual ancestors and roots, the one and same God and Father we all worship—these two faiths are indeed brother and sister. Other great religions of the world may be our cousins in the family of God, but Jews and Christians are indeed brothers and sisters.

———

Among all the things we share is one powerful, central religious and theological idea, which I would like to talk about. In many ways it is the central, formative spiritual idea or faith of both our religions, an idea which is symbolized in Judaism by the celebration of Passover, and by Christians by the celebration of Easter. You call it Passover, we call it Easter. I believe it is essentially the same message.

When, at the Passover or Seder meal, the Jewish child asks his father, "Why is this night different from all other nights?" the father, in effect, replies, "This is the night we remember that God redeems His people; that He did that when they passed over the Red Sea out of Egypt, and He is continually doing that, for He is a God of love and mercy, bringing His people out of slavery into freedom, out of darkness into light, out of pain into peace." When you eat the Passover meal, as Jesus did at the Last Supper, you recall at that most holy moment God's power to deliver us.

If I am not mistaken, that Passover celebration each year is a sign of hope—hope in God, hope that God has not deserted us, hope of the light in the darkness, hope that gives us strength to go on.

Now consider this: The most holy high moment in Christianity is Holy Week, essentially Thursday to Sunday, which commemorates how it was that Jesus, a devout Jew, on Thursday shared the Passover with his friends and said, "This bread, this wine, represents me." He identified *himself* with the Passover meaning.

And then, according to the Christian story, Jesus was killed, a victim of the human race's sin, pride, expediency, and barbarism, a martyr to the dark evil in human nature that has claimed so many victims, from the death of the Hebrew prophets, to the crucifixion of Jesus, to the horror of the Holocaust. The human race itself seems condemned by this dark and self-destructive evil that makes us capable of such incomprehensible horrors as we inflict on one another. It is as though we are slaves to this dark dance of hate, war and death.

But Christians, following in the footsteps of their Jewish forebears, claim a wonderful hope. Just as Jews claim Passover deliverance by a miraculous action of God, so Christians claim an Easter deliverance by a miraculous action of God.

Just as Jews claim that God made His move, His statement of love and mercy, power and deliverance forevermore in leading His people from Egypt, so Christians claim that God made His move, His statement of love and mercy and power and deliverance, once again, in raising Jesus from the dead.

Just as Jews claim deliverance from slavery in all its forms and live in the hope of that freedom by celebrating Passover, so Christians claim deliverance from slavery to sin and death in all its forms and live in the hope of that freedom by celebrating Easter. Essentially, as I understand it, Passover is an Easter story, and Easter is a Passover story. Exodus and Easter are the same story.

At our Holy Eucharist celebration of Easter, at the

high holy moment in the ritual, the priest holds up the unleavened bread and says, "Christ our Passover is sacrificed for us—Alleluia."

Not infrequently, of course, cynics, unbelievers, superficial critics will call our sacred faith into question and ask the question that misses the point: "Was the Red Sea really rolled back, contrary to the laws of nature?" or, "Was Jesus really risen from the dead, contrary to the laws of nature?" But the truth of Passover and Easter rests in our unshakable faith in God, in His mercy, love and forgiveness, in His power to, in the words of Isaiah the prophet in Chapter 61, "Bring good tidings to the afflicted, to bind up the brokenhearted, to proclaim liberty to the captives, the opening of the prison to those who are bound." Our faith rests in the God of Passover and Easter to bring risen life, to raise up the fallen, and make new what has become old.

Passover and Easter proclaim essentially the same message, borne out of the historical experience of our two peoples. We are linked together by an understanding of God, forged over almost 4,000 years. It is an irony, and in many ways a false turn in history, that Jesus of Nazareth has, for so many Jews and Christians, both been a symbol of separation, of misunderstanding, of difference between our people.

We are going to hear Leonard Yaseen, a devout Jew, speak on Sunday at Christ Church. His message is just such an important one—that Jesus, far from being the one who separates us, is rather the one who ought to be able to bring us together, for it is this Jesus, at the center of Christianity, who was a devout Jew, steeped in the tradition of Abraham, Isaac and Jacob, Moses and the prophets. Jesus who, rather than a stumbling block, ought somehow to be able to help provide a bridge between our great traditions. Somehow, one of God's greatest gifts to us all is the Jesus connection.

I would like to close my remarks this evening with two parables that may help us see more clearly. Both of them are true stories. The second I call the Parable of the Holly Tree.

Some years ago, in the late 1940s, Kilmer Myers, an Episcopal priest in New York City who was later to become Bishop of California, tells this true story about a Jew named Emma. Emma was a survivor of the Holocaust who lived in lower Manhattan near Kilmer Myers's church. Emma survived the Holocaust, but gravely wounded, her mind tortured by the nightmare of her experience.

Emma one day began appearing in the afternoon on the street outside of Myers's church, screaming epithets and curses about Jesus Christ and Christians. Finally Kilmer Myers went out to the street and invited Emma into the church where, perhaps, she might express her feelings more directly to Jesus. She accepted the invitation and came inside, where Father Myers left her alone for about one half hour.

Finally, returning to the church, he found her lying prostrate in the chancel in front of the great crucifix, which can be found in some Episcopal churches. He was alarmed and didn't have any idea what was happening with her. Worried, he came up to her and touched her, hoping for some response.

She looked up at him with tears in her eyes and said, "After all, he was a Jew, too, wasn't he?"

Parable of the Holly Tree

Some years ago a lovely holly tree was planted in the Christ Church cemetery and it grew large and lush and beautiful—but it never bloomed.

Twenty years later, in the 1950s, the Jewish Temple Sholom was built next door to Christ Chruch. As the new building was being landscaped, a beautiful young holly tree was planted on the grounds there.

The following year, for the first time in 20 years, and for the first time since it was planted, the holly tree in the Christ Church cemetery bloomed.

God gives us parables to help us see. May God's grace give us *all* clearer vision!

The Reverend Dr. John W. Bishop
April 18, 1986

When Neighbors Get Together

"Behold how good and how pleasant it is for brethren to dwell together in unity."

Behold how good and how pleasant it is when neighbors get together in harmony and fellowship.

Friday night was such a heart-warming experience for us next door at Temple Sholom. We were touched by your overwhelming presence and warm participation in our Sabbath evening worship. After the service, when we entered the social hall and joined hands in Israeli folk dancing with my wife Bobbie, we were making a statement of brotherhood and understanding. How wonderful when "neighbors get together" in our community.

Truly, Christ Church and Temple Sholom have enjoyed over the years a unique relationship.

As Dr. Bishop reminisced on Friday night, your first sanctuary, called Horseneck Chapel, was constructed in 1748 on the very spot that our Temple was built two hundred years later. We have always shared each other's facilities, parking lots, social halls and classrooms. Many friendships exist among the members of our congregations.

And as far as my dear friend and your Rector Dr. Jack Bishop is concerned, I am in real trouble. His Friday night sermon about Easter was so inspiring that after services one of my members approached me and said, "How about Dr. Bishop delivering the sermon every week?" And then another commented, "Why is it that your sermons are not as interesting as Dr. Bishop's?"

The story is told, probably apochryphal, that one Friday evening after the service as the Rabbi and President greeted the worshippers, a member exclaimed: "Rabbi, that was absolutely the worst sermon I ever heard. You should be ashamed of yourself!" The President was taken aback, greatly embarrassed for his spiritual leader. He put his arm around the Rabbi's shoulders and explained: "Don't listen to him, Rabbi. He only repeats what everyone else says."

Dr. Bishop observed Friday night that this was the first time in his career he had ever preached a sermon in a synagogue. However, you can visit our building across the way any Monday afternoon and find your Rector at Temple Sholom. Of course, you would not recognize him, because he is in tennis clothes, picking me up for our weekly game. Unfortunately, I rarely beat him. He plays tennis the way he preaches. Last week, when he aced me twice in one game, I rebuked him, "Jack, that was not very Christian of you."

Dr. Bishop was the catalyst for the removal of the three huge boulders separating our parking lots. He felt strongly about their incongruous presence, and by their elimination Dr. Bishop wanted to make a statement to the community that there are no barriers separating our two houses of worship. To quote the prophet Malachi, "Have we not all one father, has not one God created us all?"

Dr. Bishop spoke about Easter on Friday night. It is

my assignment this Sunday morning to discuss Passover. Your Rector developed the thesis Friday night that both Passover and Easter espouse the same essential message, that of redemption. In the case of the Christian it is redemption through Jesus. For the Jew, Passover is redemption by God from servitude.

Passover represents the call of God to the Jewish people, summoning them to freedom. Passover is comparable to the American Fourth of July, the great day of independence. True, we regard Abraham as the founder of the Jewish people. Isaac and Jacob continued the monotheistic tradition, believing in the one God, but essentially they were wandering nomads. Only during the time of Moses when we were delivered from Egypt through the miracles of the ten plagues and the crossing of the Red Sea, were we fashioned into a people. The children of Israel were the vehicle through whom God revealed himself. The Exodus from Egypt culminated at Mt. Sinai with the revelation of the Ten Commandments. Passover, then, was the beginning of the mission of the Jewish people to be, in the words of Isaiah, "a light unto the nations."

The word Passover, derived from the two words "pass" and "over," refers to the Biblical story of the Angel of Death passing over the homes of the children of Israel during the tenth plague. Passover is a family festival as is so much of the Jewish religion. The home is always regarded as the "sanctuary in miniature." The hearth is our altar; the table, our shrine; the father, high priest; the mother, high priestess; the children, communicants.

29

Passover is observed in the home at the Seder meal. Seder literally means "order," referring to the order of the service. We pray from a special book called Hagaddah, meaning "to tell" the story. As the family gathers around the table, we retell the story of the Exodus and the crossing of the Red Sea. The Seder, prefaced by asking, "Why is this night different from any other night," begins with the four questions asked by the youngest child. "Why do we eat unleavened bread? Why do we taste bitter herbs? Why do we dip twice? Why do we recline?" And now, as the Seder unfolds, the father carefully begins to answer the questions. He explains that the children of Israel were once slaves in Egypt. Moses leaves the palace, identifies with his brethren, pleads with Pharoah: "Let my people go!" With commentary and explanation, the father discusses at great length the story of the Exodus, the suffering and oppression, the ten plagues and the crossing of the Red Sea. I must relate a true story. An eight-year-old boy returned from Sunday school. His father asked the child what his teacher had explained about the forthcoming Passover festival.

The little boy answered: "As the children of Israel crossed the Red Sea, Pharoah chased them with thousands of tanks. His air force began to bomb them with jet planes. The Jewish people hastily constructed pontoon bridges and crossed the Red Sea. As soon as they reached the other side, the Israelites blew up the bridges with explosives. All the pursuing Egyptians on the bridges fell into the sea and drowned!"

"Really?" asked the astonished father. "Is that what the teacher explained was in the Bible about Passover?"

"Well, not exactly," said the little boy, "but if I told you what the Bible says about the crossing of the Red Sea, you would never believe it!"

The family Seder celebration is the opportunity for prayer and thanksgiving, for Bible study and ceremonials, spirited singing and festivity. The table is set with special food, candles, flowers and the mandatory four cups of wine. Much of the food is symbolic. The matzah or unleavened bread reminds us that there was no time for the dough to rise as the children of Israel left Egypt in haste. The radish, or bitter herbs, symbolizes the suffering of the slaves. The roast lamb represents the paschal offering. Charoset, a mixture of nuts, apples and wine, denotes the mortar that was used in the construction of the pyramids. The salt water signifies the tears that were shed as the children of Israel labored under the cruel taskmasters. The parsley indicates springtime and the festive meal.

One of the most important prayers of the Passover Seder is: "In every generation a Jew must feel that he personally participated in the Exodus." In other words, we do not merely tell the story but relive it as if "we were there." The Passover Seder, therefore, is an existential experience much the same way as your Holy Eucharist is the existential participation of the communicant in the body and blood of Jesus.

Much preparation is entailed for the Passover festival. All that is "chometz," containing bread products, is removed. The housewife carefully prepares the home in a thorough spring cleaning. Special Passover dishes, pots and cutlery replace those used during the year.

So what is the connection of Passover and Easter? Invariably, Passover and Easter occur during the same week. Why? Usually Christian holidays are observed on a specific day, as Christmas which is celebrated December 25. Only Easter is a lunar festival, occurring the first Sunday after the spring solstice. The entire Jewish calendar is lunar. Passover is always observed on the 14th, or the middle of the month, of Nisan, which is the time of spring solstice.

Historically, the Last Supper of Jesus, which occurred on a Thursday night was, in actuality, the Passover Seder. On his table were the wine and matzah, which is still an integral part of Jewish observance. The wine in the Holy Eucharist becomes the blood, and the matzah or unleavened bread, the wafer, or the body. The next day, Friday, Passover, was the crucifixion and then Sunday the resurrection.

Here is an excellent example of the Jewish-Christian connection. Jesus was a Jew. His Hebrew name was Yeshu, in Greek, Jesus. His mother was Jewish, Mary, whose Hebrew name was Miryam. Her husband was Jewish, Joseph, his Hebrew name Yosef. Paul was a Jew by the name of Shaul. Even the Apostles were Jewish as were all the early Christians.

Jesus was circumcised as a Jew, called to the Torah

as a bar mitzvah when he was thirteen and studied scriptures in the Jewish academy. On his last night, as a Jew he observed the Passover Seder. Even the eggs, which are used on Easter for the egg hunt or egg roll, are paralleled by the eggs which are the first food consumed at the Passover Seder. Why? Because eggs symbolize rebirth, rejuvenation, redemption, and hope.

After Dr. Bishop's sermon on Friday night, my wife Bobbie remarked to me: "All these years you've been saying these very same things about Christianity and Jesus and I assumed this was your opinion because you are a Rabbi; but now that Dr. Bishop is making these very same comments about the relationship of Judaism and Christianity, I am beginning to believe it!"

What a coincidence that just a few days ago, perhaps in anticipation of our services together on Friday night and Sunday morning, the Pope for the first time in history visited a synagogue in Rome. The very idea staggers the imagination. What a statement, the photograph of the Pope and the Rabbi of Rome in every newspaper throughout the world, the two of them embracing. When the Pope entered the synagogue, there was a standing ovation from the tremendous throng of worshippers. Both the Pope and the Rabbi ascended the pulpit and read together from the Book of Psalms in the original Hebrew. The Pope exclaimed: "We are brothers, you are our older brothers." In his stirring address the Pope said: "The Church deplores hatred, persecution, and displays of anti-semitism directed against the Jews at any time and by anyone. I repeat, at any time and by anyone."

Never before has any Pope ever entered a synagogue in Rome. Imagine, the Vatican is no more than a mile away from this synagogue. The Jewish community of Rome was founded two hundred years before the advent of Jesus. And now this reconciliation and rapprochement.

Certainly, there are differences between Christianity and Judaism. If there were no differences, then Christians would be Jews and Jews would be Christians. However, far more unites us than divides us. Christian and Jew believe in the same God, the same Old Testament, the same Ten Commandments and ethical and moral teachings. Judaism and Christianity are worlds apart from other major religions, Buddhism, Hinduism, Shintoism and Taoism.

On Friday night and this Sunday morning, our two congregations are making a statement—for Greenwich, for Connecticut, for our entire country. It is the identical statement enunciated by the Pope when he entered the synagogue in Rome last week. It is the statement that we members of Christ Church and Temple Sholom are proclaiming as we share this weekend of worship togehter. It is the very same statement that the founding fathers of our country promulgated when they established a republic with "liberty and justice for all," giving "to bigotry no sanction, to persecution no assistance." It is the statement declaring that each American may worship God according to the dictates of his conscience and yet live together with his fellow American in brotherhood, harmony and peace.

All that separates us is a parking lot, now that the boulders have been removed!

What a wonderful country this is, what a blessed town is Greenwich. Who would believe that an hour ago at Temple Sholom across the way, my members and I parked our automobiles in our parking lot and then, dressed in our Sunday best, walked arm in arm through your parking lot to Church.

"Behold how good and how pleasant it is for brethren to dwell together in unity."

I conclude with a parable. A theologian was asked to describe the difference between heaven and hell. He replied: "In hell millions of people, starving and emaciated, stand together. Food in abundance hangs overhead. They can reach up and touch the food; but curiously, their arms are bound at the elbow by a heavy splint, so they cannot bring the food to their mouths. In heaven you see exactly the same sight, food hanging overhead and the peoples' arms bound at the elbow by a splint. And yet, they are not starving, they are full and satiated. True, they cannot bring the food to their mouths. But in heaven they bring the food to their neighbor's mouths.

"And now," he concluded, "you understand. The basic difference between heaven and hell is a helping hand, cooperation, a little bit of tolerance and understanding."
Amen.

Dr. Hillel E. Silverman
April 20, 1986

The Jewish-Christian Connection

Thank you . . . for your vision in initiating this program, defying conventional, safe tradition in your quest for a more rational world. Thank you, Dr. Bishop, for the opportunity of communicating with two congregations in this beautiful church today. I have enjoyed Rabbi Silverman's outstanding sermon.

In little more than a decade all Christiandom will celebrate an historic event—the 2,000th year since the birth of Jesus. His life was tragically brief. His crucifixion was witnessed only by a handful of followers and mocking Roman soldiers. Yet his death has profoundly influenced the course of history.

Missionaries for Jesus have traversed the globe: Immense cathedrals have been constructed in His name; sculptures, paintings and murals have been dedicated to His eternal glorification. The grim instrument of His execution, the cross, has been lovingly symbolized in billions of gold, silver, stone and wood reproductions.

Existence in an earlier, troubled world meant struggling without dignity or security, a fertile atmosphere for the spiritual comfort inherent in the teachings of Jesus. Now, almost a billion Christians constitute powerful religious bodies dominating North and South America, Europe, Australia and portions of Asia and Africa.

As we approach the year 2000, many denominations devoted to Jesus Christ embrace and worship Him in separate ways, leading frequently to cruel divisiveness. Jesus proclaimed a gospel of love. Tragically, many who call themselves Christian transformed His teachings into a gospel of denigration for Jesus's own people, his own flesh and blood. Centuries of such indoctrination have resulted in degradation and even genocide. In this country alone, the lives of millions of innocent men, women and children have been shattered by mindless anti-Semitism.

However, after nineteen hundred years of persecution we are now witnessing a remarkable reversal in the volatile history of Judaic-Christian relations. The very same Church that alienated Jesus from His Jewish family and sought frequently to impose its belief through coercion, has now come forth with a policy of ecumenical respect toward Jews and Judaism.

The late, revered Pope John XXIII has driven out most of the demonic phantoms of the past, making it possible for Jews to gain new understanding from the life and meaning of Jesus, certainly one of their most illustrious kinsmen. And he has made it possible for Christians to learn more about their roots in Judaism. Yes, Pope John XXIII is one of the reasons we are here in this beautiful church, communicating cordially and candidly: two congregations expressing good will—exactly what Jesus meant when he said "Love thy neighbor as thyself."

I wrote *The Jesus Connection* to encourage better relations between Christians and Jews. Can you imagine how overjoyed I am that this modest book has been the instrument that brings us together today? Of course, many positive, thoughtful actions have preceded this meeting, but before we can talk about that good news, let's put the past in proper perspective so that we can help build a firm and brighter future in harmony.

To accomplish that we need to strip away the cobwebs and choking dust of centuries of misconceptions about Christianity, Judaism and Jesus, and reveal the danger of bigotry to persons of all religions.

We might begin with the realization that most of us know very little about one another. Father Theodore Hesburgh, president of Notre Dame University, in his introduction to *The Jesus Connection*, observes, "To build bridges across the gap of mutual ignorance and suspicion we will have to return to origins to recover those common threads with which we can hope to have a fresh shared identity."

Our shared identity begins in the first century. There were no miracle medicines then to cure or ease the pain or almost certain death from leprosy, smallpox, tuberculosis, or myriad other diseases. There were no scientific explanations for the mysterious forces of nature. People existed in the foul grip of abject poverty. The Jews, oppressed by the brutal Roman Empire, stood alone as ethical monotheists in a sea of pagan nations. It was a time of overwhelming tyranny, superstition, unrest and apprehension.

To many Jews, Jesus of Nazareth was the answer

to their prayer of overthrowing Roman domination. Jesus was of the tribe of Judah, linked to David, Abraham, and Moses. A Jewish mother, Mary, nursed him. Joseph taught him a carpenter's skills. Despite these humble beginnings, he became known as a great teacher, and talk of his mysterious powers accompanied him everywhere.

It is assumed that Jesus repudiated Judaism, originated an entirely new religious concept, founded Christianity, was rejected by his fellow Jews.

Did Jesus ever renounce Judaism? He was born, lived, and died as a Jew. He never heard the word "Christianity." The only bible Jesus read was the Hebrew bible and the prophets of Israel. His teachings were all based on Hebrew scriptures and traditions.

Did not Jesus denounce the high priest and the goings-on in the temple? The high priest probably deserved his censure. But criticizing the religious hierarchy of his day was no more anti-Jewish than Luther or Calvin were anti-Christian in their disapproval of certain actions of the Church. Which of us has not found fault with the establishment—religious or secular? We don't go along with everything—does that make us less American? Did that make Jesus less Jewish?

Did the Jews collectively reject Jesus? His disciples were all Jews. So were John the Baptist and all the early bishops and saints. His fellow Jews with whom he came in contact loved and accepted Him. Most Jews did not even live in the Holy Land at the time of Jesus—they had dispersed over a period of 500 years

39

before his death. A "national" Jewish policy would have been impossible.

Did Jesus preach Christianity? His Jewish followers founded a new sect of Judaism which eventually became Christianity.

Jewish-Christian services were held in Jewish synagogues forty years after Jesus's death. There were no churches then. Christian services today are still patterned on synagogue customs and convictions: the concepts of heaven and hell, the Psalms, the words amen and hallelujah, the Lord's Prayer and baptism, the belief in a Messiah, and resurrection. The Last Supper was a Passover celebration. Jesus's penultimate words on the cross—"My God, my God, why hast thou forsaken me?"—were from the 22nd Psalm.

The temple in Jerusalem with its brilliantly attired clergymen, beautiful lace-covered altar, music and incense, prayer shawls and head coverings served as the inspiration for central features of later Christian churches.

Well, what happened to change the course of history? What was the parting of the ways?

Several events created a turning point in Christian-Jewish relations. The Romans destroyed Jerusalem and the citizens who had remained in tiny Judea, the only nation that believed in one God, were now completely dispersed, scattered, no longer considered a factor in history. In order to expand Christianity, religious leaders needed to convert Greeks, Syrians, Romans, and others. However, pagans strenuously objected to adult circumcision

40

required under Jewish law. The church elders decided to eliminate this requirement in order to enlarge the new faith and, in the process, began to distance themselves from Judaism.

Simultaneously, many Jews felt they had to turn away from the new faith because Paul, on the road to Damascus, testified that in a blinding flash of light he had heard Jesus speak to him as the Lord who was divine. Many Jews were sympathetic to Jesus as a Messiah but their commitment to a monotheistic god, one Father in heaven, made it impossible for them to accept His divinity.

As the new doctrine was taken out of the synagogue, Christianity gravitated toward Rome. But there was no welcoming committee. From Caesar down, Christians were treated barbarically—massacred, tortured, and burned at the stake. As a small sect, Christianity was entirely dependent on the good will of Roman authorities for its very existence. Over the next several hundred years a furious battle raged between Christianity and the formidable power of the Roman Empire. Persecution of the new faith never ceased, churches were demolished and religious materials, including original gospel documents, confiscated and burned. Only when the Roman emperor Constantine officially established toleration for Christianity in 313 A.D. was Christian sacred literature encouraged to surface again.

The New Testament was compiled by men of humble origin toward the end of the first century A.D. as Christianity was attempting to gain this foothold in Rome.

———

The Gospels reinforced the new religion by appeasing the Romans and blaming the Jews for the crucifixion of Jesus. Portions of the New Testament emphasize differences between Christianity and its mother religion, stigmatize Judaism and, in particular, diminish the Jewishness of Jesus. There was probably a practical reason. Rome had crushed a Jewish rebellion against its tyranny. Jesus was perceived as a rebel whose followers were a threat to Caesar's power and divinity. Why should Christians remind Rome that Jesus was a Jew? Better to separate Him from His people. They achieved that result.

Reshaping events already veiled by the passage of time is confirmed by Father John Hardon, an eminent historian. In his book *Christianity in the Twentieth Century,* he observes that the Gospels had a tendency to "obscure and embellish, if not distort, the facts to meet the demands of an idealistic new faith" so that religious instruction, constantly repeated, conditioning successive generations with mythical arguments, became part of history. After hundreds of years, myths take on the semblance of reality and are accepted as events that happened exactly as portrayed.

The notion that the Jews are collectively responsible for the death of Jesus, their fellow Jew, is the single most damaging accusation that has afflicted any people anywhere, anytime.

If we interpret the Gospels dispassionately, many sections indicate that Jews were not responsible for His death. Mark 14:2 says, "We can not sentence him *or there will be a riot."* (Emphasis added.) Luke 19:47–48 says, "Caiaphas sought to destroy him and could not *for all the people were attentive to him."* (Emphasis added.) In Matthew 27:17–18 we find, "The high priest envied Jesus and had him arrested *because of his popularity with the people."* (Emphasis added.)

Obviously, his Jewish followers loved and accepted Jesus. Still another misconception is clarified in the gospel of John—he established that Jesus was *not* put on trial before the Sanhedrin, the Supreme Court of Judea. There was no gathering of all the judges of the Holy Land and there was no trial. Under Jewish law no crime had been committed. Claiming messiahship was not unusual—dozens of people before Jesus had claimed to be messiahs. John 18:13–15 confirms only Caiaphas and his father-in-law interviewed Jesus before he was turned over to Pontius Pilate.

Two persons seem to share responsiblity for Jesus's crucifixion—the Jewish high priest Caiaphas and the Roman procurator Pontius Pilate.

Did Caiaphas represent the Jewish populace? Absolutely not! He was so hated that the people of Jerusalem burned down his home in the great revolt of 66 A.D. As a Roman collaborator he could not be termed a Jewish leader at all. He was appointed by Rome, was loyal only to Rome, did the will of Rome, and could immediately be removed by Rome. We must remember that the Holy Land was enslaved by the Roman Empire and freedom of choice was unknown. Caiaphas could not make a single independent decision, conduct a service, or officiate at a meeting without Roman instruction. Even his robe, his vestments, were kept in the office of Romans.

The Gospels depict Pontius Pilate, Caesar's representative, as a faint-hearted weakling merely acquiescing to the Jews in the crucifixion of Jesus. Historians of his day more accurately describe Pilate as insolent, rapacious and cruel, universally recognized for corruptibility and violence. He was known to line the roads of Judea with crucified Jews, sent to death on the barest hint of "revolutionary" attitudes. Jesus was one of these. Pilate was so brutal that even Rome could not take him for long, and he was recalled in disgrace because of his excesses.

Eugene J. Fisher of the National Conference of Catholic Bishops observes that "the Gospels portray a kindly ruler (Pilate) pushed by Jews into killing Jesus. Since they were written at a time when the survival of the Church depended on Roman tolerance, it is understandable that Pilate's role be played down."

According to the late Dr. Bernhard Olsen, a Methodist scholar, many churches throughout the world continue to teach the same story so that countless children begin life with a prejudice—the Jews who killed Jesus 2,000 years ago, they are told, are the same as those who live in the next block.

Atheists in Russia have appropriated these centuries-old images, repackaged them and translated them into forms such as anti-Zionism. Today in Moscow a so-called center for Zionist information distributes vast amounts of vicious propaganda for use by Libya, Saudi Arabia and Syria who in turn supply this ammunition to racist and hate groups in this country.

44

One of the most troublesome domestic crises today is that of the farmers and our food supply. How in the world did that become an issue of anti-Semitism? For two principal reasons: 1) Professional rabblerousers deliberately blamed "the Jews" and 2) many farmers believed this accusation because the seeds of prejudice were planted centuries ago—and that kind of indoctrination can't be wiped out overnight. The idea of Jewish bankers foreclosing on farm mortgages is absurd—there are no major Jewish banks. They are controlled by non-Jews and always have been.

Still another canard is that the Jews control the print and electronic media. A recent study documents that of the 1,700 U.S. newspapers, over 96 percent are controlled by non-Jews. NBC is owned by General Electric. ABC is controlled by Americans of Irish descent, CBS is run by persons of every denomination and the principal cable networks are operated by a fellow named Ted Turner, a born-again Christian.

When a black muslim preacher, paid millions of dollars by an Arab dictator who happens to be the world's leading terrorist, calls Judaism a gutter religion and incites 25,000 people in an audience to rise up and scream invectives, that's anti-Semitism and it's happening now.

At this moment I can understand how some of you might be getting a little fed up with talk about Jews, anti-Semitism, early Rome and so forth. You may well wonder how all this applies to you when, in fact, the people in this audience are basically of good will.

But outside this handsome edifice and away from this enlightened environment are forces whose hos-

45

tility threatens all of us. Need I tell this informed audience what a serious threat religious fanaticism and hatred are to world stability today? Verbal aggression is dangerous because it accelerates into physical violence. And genocidal doctrines based on fury and bigotry against one group have a boomerang effect and eventually encompass all groups.

The tragic consequences of the Spanish inquisition are a case in point. In the beginning, the Spanish monarchy, with an inquisitor appointed by the Catholic Church, persecuted Jews and Moors, but soon Protestants were tortured and burned for refusing to adhere to the strictures of Catholic orthodoxy. Eventually, Catholics themselves were jeopardized, thousands imprisoned and put to death as heretics. Ultimately, no one was above suspicion. In a single day a Catholic family could be stripped of all its possessions merely because of a fancied slight to an official of the all-powerful Inquisition. As for Spain, by the mid 1600s its glory was only a memory, its powerful fleet disbanded, its people in ferment, its economy in ruins. Spain was no longer among the powerful nations of the world—a credo of hate had destroyed its unity.

Are lessons learned from disasters like this? In Europe, country after country has experienced this kind of devastation. The latest example, Germany, cost the lives of more than 20 million people, left a shattered continent and a divided country.

For two centuries America has carefully maintained its secular and religious distinctions and provided us with previously unheard of individual rights and freedoms. It is this dualism that has made America the great bastion of civil, political and religious liberties.

Since Vatican II, church leaders of every denomination have condemned anti-Semitism. The United Methodists state: "It is not enough for Christians to be aware of our common origins. They are also obligated to examine their own responsibility for discrimination and organized extermination of Jews." The Lutheran World Federation observes: "Lutherans of today refuse to be bound by Luther's attacks on the Jews." The World Council of Churches states: "The Church must preach the gospel so as to make sure that it cannot be used toward contempt for Judaism or the Jewish people."

The Jesus Connection contains a number of personal vignettes illustrating how attitudes are improving—how Christians in this century have risked their careers and their lives to help others in the true spirit of Christianity.

To illustrate the absurdity of stereotyping, I have included in the book photographs and brief biographies of Jewish people who have enriched our shared universe: medical pioneers who established the first blood bank, developed streptomycin, digitalis, insulin and polio vaccines; television and film performers like Shatner and Nimoy of *Star Trek*, Michael Landon, Lorne Greene, Joan Collins, Kirk Douglas, Cary Grant, Debra Winger and Tony Randall. Musicians and writers like Theodore White, Tom Stoppard, Victor Borge, Billy Joel, Bob Dylan, Dinah Shore, and Beverly Sills. Public servants like

Arthur Burns, Harold Brown, William Paley, Admiral Hyman Rickover, and giants of the past, Einstein and Freud, and those with one Jewish parent — Fiorello LaGuardia, Douglas Fairbanks and others.

In our day to day existence Jews are no better or no worse than others. And physically, not all Jews resemble Paul Newman or Paulette Goddard than all Christians compare favorably with Robert Redford and Meryl Streep.

The Jesus Connection is my effort to contribute to a growing tradition of mutual respect, the keystone of democratic pluralism. With this background, parents and teachers can help future generations reject bigotry, discard stereotypes, explore the common roots of Christianity and Judaism, and tell the truth about Jesus's Jewish heritage.

Jews, on their part, must understand that Jesus can be appreciated as a great teacher and prophet. Father Theodore Hesburgh observes that "belief in the divinity of Jesus expressly affirms our recognition of his full humanity—as a Jew." It is erroneous for Jews to equate Jesus with extreme elements in the past responsible for Jewish humiliation, persecution, and near annihilation.

The noted Israeli historian Pinchas Lapide has said, "What united us is everything that is known and investigated with the tools of scholarship about Jesus. What divides us are the things that divide not only Jews from Christians but also knowledge from faith. . . .Faith in this Christ has given millions a better life and an easier death. With Christians the fullness of redemption is still in the future. If the

---

Messiah comes and turns out to be Jesus of Nazareth I do not know any Jew in this world who would have anything against it."

Today we face monumental problems demanding the brain power, judgment and dedication of all citizens of our composite society. People, not oil or technology are the greatest resource. Is it not utterly foolish to waste human assets because of differences in how we pray to the same God?

The world is moving too fast. We have trouble communicating our values. We are bewildered by international terrorism, the constant threat to our society, and by violent crime in our streets.

H.G. Wells has written that "civilization is ultimately a race between education and destruction." Together we can make a contribution to helping America and the human family win the battle of reciprocal esteem over bigotry, of love over hatred, and to affirm our shared conviction that every human being is the precious child of God.

Recently I read an excerpt of a sermon by a Presbyterian minister which summarizes our meeting today. He observed, "In that time, when our need is greatest to feel Christ with us, when death approaches us or one we love, we turn again to Jewish scripture: 'The Lord is my shepherd, I shall not want. . . . Yea, though I walk through the Valley of the Shadow of Death, I will fear no evil. For Thou art with me . . . '"

Leonard Yaseen
April 20, 1986

The Next Step: What You Can Do

As a lay member of a congregation:

Share this book with your clergyman. Discuss with him the possibility of arranging a similar program with a neighboring church or synagogue.

As a clergyman:

Consider using this book as a guide for: 1) a weekend service with a neighboring church or synagogue; 2) a study program for church and temple activities: youth groups, women's organizations, Bible study classes, child and adult Sunday school, confirmation classes, social groups.

As a member of an organization:

Speak to your chairman about arranging a program or series of programs on the subject of this book.

As a parent or godparent:

At mealtimes, on walks, at quiet moments, introduce children to the ideas this book contains.

On a personal level:

Give an informal lunch or dinner party for your friends where you can discuss the theme of this book.

The Contributors

The Rev. John Wesley Bishop, D. Min., became Rector of Christ Church in November 1982.

Born in Kingston, New York, where his great-grandfather John Wesley Bishop was a Methodist circuit rider and preacher, Dr. Bishop graduated from Phillips Andover Academy, and in 1950 from Yale University. He served two years in the U.S. Marine Corps.

After receiving a Master of Divinity degree from Virginia Theological Seminary in 1954, the year he was ordained an Episcopal clergyman, Dr. Bishop served for two years as Assistant Minister at the Church of the Redeemer in Cincinnati, Ohio. From 1954–1956 he was chaplain of Cincinnati Children's Hospital. He then began the Mission of St. Timothy's Church in Cincinnati. He spent a sabbatical leave in 1967 as an Industrial Chaplain and Scholar on Church Renewal at Coventry Cathedral, England. In 1971, after fifteen years at St. Timothy's, during which he brought that mission to parish status, he accepted a call to be Rector of St. Thomas' Church, Rochester, New York.

In his eleven years at St. Thomas' Dr. Bishop served as clergy advisor to the Genesee Valley Hospice Program, taught a course in pastoral care at Colgate/Rochester Bexley Hall Seminary, and worked in the community as an accredited Clinical Member and Supervisor of the American Association of Marriage and Family Therapists. In 1976 he received his Doctorate of Ministry in Marriage and Family Counseling at Colgate/Rochester Bexley Hall.

His wife Jo-Ann, a graduate of Vassar College with advanced degrees in art history from Yale and the University of Cincinnati, was Curator of Oriental Art at the the Strong Museum in Rochester. A particular interest was the Rochester Interfaith Jail Ministry.

Dr. and Mrs. Bishop have four sons.

* * *

Dr. Hillel E. Silverman has been Rabbi of Temple Sholom since 1981.

Born in Hartford, Connecticut, he is the son of the late Rabbi and Mrs. Morris Silverman. His father was the spiritual leader of the Emanuel Synagogue in Hartford for fifty years, and a nationally known author and compiler of numerous prayer books. Mrs. Silverman was a well-known author.

Dr. Silverman graduated from Yale with highest honors, and studied at the Hebrew University in Jerusalem. He was ordained a Rabbi at the Jewish Theological Seminary of America where, in 1952, he received his Doctorate in the field of Bible. Entering the U.S. Navy as chaplain in 1951, he served in Naples, Italy, for the Mediterranean Sixth Fleet and NATO Shore Establishments in that area. Dr. Silverman is a Full Commander in the U.S. Naval Reserve.

During his ministry from 1954–1964 at Congregation Shearith Israel in Dallas, Texas, he developed a multi-faceted educational and youth program. From 1964–1980 Dr. Silverman served the Sinai Temple in Los Angeles. A frequent traveler to Israel, he was awarded the Prime Minister's Medal for distinguished service to Israel and the Jewish people, and in 1978 he received the Israel Service Medal.

Among his numerous activities Rabbi Silverman served on the executive committee and as past national chairman of the United Jewish Appeal Rabbinical Cabinet, the Israel Bonds Rabbinical Cabinet, the national advisory committee of the Jewish National Fund, the Commission on Jewish Chaplaincy, and as past president of the Zionist Organization of America, Southwest Region. His current duties include director of the American Friends of Hebrew, Tel Aviv, and Ben Gurion Universities; and National Deputy Chaplain, Jewish War Veterans of America. Locally he serves on the board of directors of the Greenwich Jewish Federation, Jewish Community Service, and the American Red Cross. He is a panel member of cable television's "The Other Side of the News."

Dr. Silverman is the author of a number of books and has contributed articles to such publications as *Jewish Spectator, Jewish Digest* (where he is a member of the editorial advisory board), *Conservative Judaism, United Synagogue Review,* and *American Rabbi.* He is listed in a number of directories, including Who's Who in Religion, International Authors and Writers Who's Who, Who's Who in Israel, International Who's Who of Intellectuals, and Men of Achievement.

Dr. Silverman is married and has three children.

*   *   *

Leonard C. Yaseen, author of *The Jesus Connection,* (New York: The Crossroad Publishing Co.), is the retired founder of the Fantus Company, an international consulting firm that relocates companies that need to move or to build facilities in a new area.

Mr. Yaseen began Fantus in 1934 and sold it to Dun & Bradstreet in 1966, remaining as chairman until his retirement in 1971. His company relocated thousands of facilities and millions of employees. His clients included such Fortune 500 organizations as Mobil, Texaco, Westinghouse, Borden and Nabisco.

In negotiating over 5,000 moves during his career, Mr. Yaseen and Fantus created millions of new jobs, established training schools to bring untrained people into the marketplace and at the same time stressed the need for racially integrated industrial operations.

The author of four texts on industrial economic geography, Mr. Yaseen and his wife Helen live in Westchester County, New York, and Palm Beach, Florida. Their common interest in art led them to found the Yaseen Studies in Modern Art at the Metropolitan Museum of Art in New York and the Yaseen Lectures at the Neuberger Museum in Purchase, New York.

Mr. Yaseen in also a trustee of the Hirshorn Museum of the Smithsonian Institution and of the State University of New York at Purchase.

(l. to r.), Rabbi Hillel E. Silverman, Leonard
Yaseen, and the Rev. John W. Bishop.

Last Words

From the Psalms of David

33:12 Blessed is the nation whose God is
      the Lord,
    the people he chose for his
      inheritance.

33:13 From heaven the Lord looks down
    and sees all mankind.

33:14 from his dwelling place he watches
    all who live on earth—

33:15 he who forms the hearts of all
    who considers everything they do.

33:16 No king is saved by the size of his
      army;
    No warrior escapes by his great
      strength.

33:17 A horse is a vain hope for
      deliverance;
    despite all its great strength it
      cannot save.

33:18 But the eyes of the Lord are on those
      who fear him,
    on those whose hope is in his
      unfailing love,

33:19 to deliver them from death
    and keep them alive in famine.

33:20   We wait in hope for the Lord;
        he is our help and our shield.

33:21   In him our hearts rejoice,
        for we trust in his holy name.

33:22   May your unfailing love rest upon us,
        O Lord,
        even as we put our hope in you.

From the Proverbs of Solomon

3:27 Do not withhold good from those
      who deserve it,
    when it is in your power to act.

3:29 Do not plot harm against your
      neighbor,
    who lives trustfully near you.

3:30 Do not accuse a man for no reason—
    when he has done you no harm.

4:14 Do not set foot on the path of the
      wicked
    or walk in the way of evil men.

4:15 Avoid it, do not travel on it;
    turn from it and go on your way.

4:16 For they cannot sleep till they do evil;
    they are robbed of slumber till they
      make someone fall.

4:17 They eat the bread of wickedness
    and drink the wine of violence,

4:18 The path of the righteous is like the
      first gleam of dawn,
    shining ever brighter till the full
      light of day.

5:12 Hatred stirs up dissension,
    but love covers over all wrongs.

5:17 He who heeds discipline shows the
      way to life,
    but whoever ignores correction
      leads others astray.

Matthew 5:23, 24

So if you are offering your gift at the altar, and there remember that your brother has something against you, leave your gift there before the altar and go; first be reconciled to your brother, and then come and offer your gift.

The Lord's Prayer

Our Father, Which art in heaven,
Hallowed be Thy name.
Thy kingdom come,
Thy will be done,
On earth as it is in Heaven.
Give us this day our daily bread
And forgive us our trespasses
As we forgive those who trespass against us.
And lead us not into temptation
But deliver us from evil
For Thine is the Kingdom and the power
 and the glory, forever and ever.
Amen.

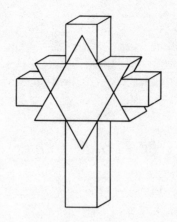

Acknowledgment

This book was published with a grant from the Arnold and Marie Schwartz Fund for Education and Health Research.

DATE DUE